The Guyana Business Law Overview

The Power of Attorney Act

Written by

Brenden Glasford

Edited by Jarienn James

Published by Zenith Inc

Croal Street, Georgetown. Guyana.

ISBN 978-976-97721-1-3 (Paperback)

Disclaimer

The content which forms this book is solely for educational purposes.

The views of the author are his interpretation of Guyanese Legislation but are not to be considered legal advice.

Legal advice must be sought from an Attorney-at-Law based on the facts of your particular situation.

Dedication

To my wife, your support and faith is an inspiration.

To my children, I keep writing to show you it's important to –

– never stop learning, no matter how old you are.

Table of Contents

Contents

Part I – Introductory Themes

1. Laws & Facts

"Good legislation should bring clarity not confusion"

– Bill Haslam

The beginning of Statutory Agency

The Power of Attorney Act[1] is law that predates the existence of Guyana by just about three decades. It is an artifice of British Guiana, passed by the Colonial Legislature on 14 May 1932. It stayed unchanged for decades, until a series of high profile transactions came to light and required action by the Legislature.

[1] Chapter 5:08 of the Laws of Guyana

Impetus for Amendment – Egregious fraudulent transactions

The first amendment of the Power of Attorney Act occurred on 14 January 2022, just ten years shy of a century after its enactment in 1932.

It's quite amazing that a piece of legislation that governs instruments that are used daily to facilitate business and personal transactions didn't need amending before its 90th anniversary. This fact speaks volumes about our regulatory culture, without saying a word.

I have read several cases and heard countless anecdotes during the course of my legal practice, about powers of attorney being used for fraudulent purposes. I am sure that if our society's collective memory is consulted, it will reveal that this type of use of Powers has been a problem since the legislation's inception. Our society must do significantly better in addressing known issues through legislation or regulation in a timely manner.

A case decided by the Caribbean Court of Justice (CCJ) highlights the issue quite well. The case[2] was decided on February 2021. This concerned a power that was drafted, executed and recorded without the individual who purportedly granted it, Mr. Allan Price, who was not present at the time of the instrument's execution, nor was he aware of the creation of the instrument. The purported agent appointed by the instrument, Jennifer Jeboo, used the power to sell Mr. Price's land in Queenstown, Georgetown to Ms. Marlene Todd. The fraud was subsequently discovered, alas, after Mr. Price had died. It fell to the executrix of his estate to attempt recovery of the property transferred by fraud. The matter meandered its way through the Court system making it to the top of the judicial mountain, the CCJ. It is really because of the decision of the CCJ in this matter that the law saw amendment.

Less than a year after the decision of the CCJ, the Legislature amended the Act to deal with instances of impersonation of a person granting authority or an individual being able to execute

---

[2] Todd v Price and Jeboo [2021] CCJ 2

and record an instrument without the knowledge and approval of the party granting the power.

However, the legislators missed an important opportunity, putting provisions in place to stop unscrupulous agents from breaching their fiduciary duties and taking advantage of their position to benefit themselves and/or third parties.

A recent case[3] of the High Court in Guyana has highlighted this type of unscrupulous behaviour of a properly appointed agent. In this particular case, a mother granted her son agency, and he went on to transfer immovable property to himself. The Court's finding was that the agent's actions were a breach of trust reposed in him when his mother granted him the power[4] for him to transfer the property to himself without his mother's express permission.

---

[3] Pharsi v Pharsi
[4] Paras [15] and [16]

2. Purpose & Caution

"To forget one's purpose is the commonest form of stupidity"

– Friedrich Nietzsche

Purpose

In the preamble of the Act. It states, "An Act to make provision with respect to the recording of Powers of Attorney, their effect and their revocation." This statement while accurate in substance falls short in detail. Let us consider some more of the details, where appointing an agent by a Power of Attorney is concerned.

A note on nomenclature

Readers will note the use of the terms "grantor" and "grantee", when discussing the parties whose names appear on the power of attorney document. The terms "principal" and "agent" are also used. For the avoidance of doubt, allow me to provide a short explanation presently.

The use of the terms “Grantor” and “Principal” can be used interchangeably. These terms refer to a person who will give or has given his authority to another person to do some task or tasks on his behalf.

While the terms “Grantee” and “Agent” are used to refer to the person who receives the authority and acts on behalf of the Grantor of the Power.

You may notice in the Act, use of the words “Donor” and “Donee”. I disapprove of the use of the terms as those terms usually refer to the granting of a gift. They should not be used to describe the individuals granting or receiving the authority.

In the Guyana context, the use of any word that implies the granting of agency is a gift should be frowned upon. As such I choose not to use the term and favour the other terms set out above.

The Nature of Powers in Guyana

In Guyana, powers are limited by the capacity of the person granting it. This means if the person loses his authority to act on his own behalf, the agent no longer has the power conferred. This can be caused by his death, lunacy, insolvency or bankruptcy.

In other parts of the world. For example, in the United States of America, there are powers which are "durable" and can survive the loss of capacity of the person who grants the agent the power to act on his behalf. These are especially useful for caring for older people and estate planning while a principal may still be alive but has lost the capacity to make decisions and/or act for himself.

The Business Significance of Powers

There is no instrument of greater utility in business circumstances than the instrument that creates Agency. It allows an individual to be in two places at once, granting the rarest of all gifts – *more time*.

It allows you to take action on behalf of your business in one place while your agent takes action on behalf of your business in another place, adding a multiplier of efficiency to your business.

Use of Powers by Legal Persons

While individuals benefit significantly from the strategic use of Powers. Companies gain even greater benefits. The directorate of the company can appoint different agents to act on its behalf in different capacities.

However, giving power in a commercial context is an action that should only be taken after careful consideration and discussion with the employee or officer the company plans to use, especially if the tasks fall outside of the scope of that employee's or officer's job description. Another consideration is, can this person be trusted to act autonomously?

If used judiciously it can allow a company to appoint more agents, multiplying its productivity.

Ex abundanti cautela [5]

When appointing an Agent, a Grantor must bear in mind that an instrument of agency can be just as dangerous as it is useful. There are not too many recorded cases that you can find on the issue. You will hear stories of matters which never rose to the level of the Courts. The stories tell of powers, although properly executed and recorded in accordance with the law, used by the agent in breach of fiduciary duties.

It is incumbent that the Grantor act out of an abundance of caution when considering the appointment of his agent, even someone he knows well. The Grantor must have a frank discussion with the prospective agent about the duties the agency will require of him. It is critical for the agent to understand the nature and extent of the agency, the risk that the agent may face and any other relevant facts or circumstances. Due diligence may also require the formation of a contract of agency to set out terms, conditions and

---

[5] From an abundance of caution

payment. Agency can be onerous to the agent and adequate compensation should be a normal feature in agency arrangements.

Part II – Legislative Tenets

3. Execution

"What we can control is our performance and our execution, and that what we're going to focus on."

– Bill Belichick

The process of execution of Powers of Attorney and establishing of the identity of the parties thereto has been a major theme of the 2022 amendment. The rationale being that a case like **Todd v Jeboo** should never reoccur, if they tightened up the identity requirements.

Execution - Both parties are in the same country

The changes to the execution of powers set out in the 2022 amendment now require both parties whose names appear on the power to present themselves before the notary public with the following documents:

1. The power of Attorney document.
2. Two photo ID documents and color copies of those photo ID documents to be verified by the Notary and attached to the executed power.

Once they appear with those documents, they are required to sign the power in the presence of two witnesses. After which the two witnesses are to sign the document. After the document has been signed the Notary will notarize the document and the photo ID copies.

Execution - Both parties are in different countries

Where the grantor of the power is outside of Guyana and wishes to appoint an agent to act on his behalf inside Guyana, he must execute the document in the following manner. He must appear before a Notary Public, preferably at a Consulate of Guyana. He will appear with two forms of photo ID which will be presented before the Notary Public. He must sign the document before the

Notary Public and two witnesses. The Notary Public will then proceed to Notarize the document and the copies of the Photo ID.

Once complete the Grantor must send the document to the Grantee for the process to be completed in Guyana. This will entail the Grantee visiting a Notary Public in Guyana with two forms of Photo ID and signing the document in the presence of two witnesses. Once this is done the Notary Public in Guyana will notarize the document and the copies of the photo ID. The grantee can proceed to record the document once they have completed this step.

4. Recording

"Life is like a cash register, in that every account, every thought, every deed, like every sale, is registered and recorded"

– Fulton J. Sheen

What is taken

With the execution of the instrument complete, the Grantor or Grantee as the case may be, must consider the recording of the document.

The term "record" refers to the process of registration of the document with the regulatory authority, the Deeds Registry.

The document cannot be used before it is recorded by the Deeds Registry. It is only after the instrument has been recorded that the Agency begins. Allowing the agent to act on his principal's behalf.

The process of recording a Power is straightforward, although it can be time consuming, depending on the foot traffic inside the Registry. Before entering the Registry to record the instrument, make sure that you have at least two copies of the Power of Attorney and all attendant documents, as the registry will keep the original copy.

After you finish waiting in line to speak to a registry representative, the representative will ask to see the documents. They will then check to ensure that the following essential particulars are in order:

- The names of the Grantor and Grantee.
- The photocopies of the 2 forms of photo ID.
- The signatures of the Grantor and Grantee.
- The signatures of the witnesses.
- The signature and stamp of the notary on the instrument.
- The signature and stamp of the notary on the photo IDs.

Once the representative has determined that the documents meet the statutory requirements, the document will be taxed. The term "taxed" is the term used to describe calculating the cost of the document. Once payment is made, the Registry will accept the documents to start the recording process and the person who filed the document will be given a receipt and told when to return for the recorded instrument.

What is uplifted

When a person goes to uplift the instrument the following additions to the document should be noted. The additions indicate that the document collected is a properly recorded and valid Power of Attorney. The additions are:

- At the top of the document, you should notice 8 handwritten numbers. These numbers indicate the number and year of the Power of Attorney. For instance, if the instrument bears the number 5869/2025 this means that the document is the 5869th instrument registered in the year

2025. This is a useful number to recall, should you lose the Power and need another copy or need to reference it for some reason.

- On the top right hand corner there will be the taxing information which is proof that the document went through the taxing process in the Deeds Registry.

•

5. Duration

"In short, you can't let the deadline define the mission. The mission has to define the duration"

– Richard Holbrooke

Powers of Attorney can be created to last as long as the Grantor/ Donor wishes and only loses validity in the following cases:

- The Grantor loses capacity by death, lunacy, insolvency or bankruptcy.
- The Grantor decides to revoke the power.
- The Grantee renounces the office of Agent.
- The Grantee dies.

The Act also allows for powers to exist for a limited time. This is not a common practice in Guyana, but it should be used more often. It could save a principal a great deal of trouble if the agent's authority did not linger for longer than necessary. As the good books says, "Idle hands are the devil's workshop[6]". It can also create a much needed sense of urgency in completing the tasks which can increase efficiency. To Limit the duration of an instrument, the time restriction must be placed on the document for all to clearly see and read.

---

[6] Proverbs Chapter 16 Verse 27

6. Authority's End

"Every Choice is Renunciation. Indeed, every Choice is a thousand renunciations. To choose one thing is to turn one's back on many others."

– Ronald Rolheiser

Revoking a Power of Attorney

There may come a time when a principal does not wish for his agent to continue to act on his behalf. This can happen for a number of reasons. It may be that the task or transaction has come to an end. It could also be that the principal has lost confidence in the agent, or a myriad of other less common reasons.

Whatever the reason, revocation must be done by the Grantor of the Power of Attorney. The revocation must be done in writing, by filing a notarized record of the revocation in the Deeds Registry. This will entail the grantor taking a drafted revocation to a notary and having it notarized and then filed with the Deeds Registry. Once this document is filed the Deeds Registry copy of the Power will be stamped "Revoked" with the details of the document revoking it.

Revocation can also be triggered by the death, unsoundness of mind or insolvency of the Grantor. If any of these circumstances are brought to the attention of the Registrar or Deputy Registrar of Deeds, either of those officers can have it annotated on the Power of Attorney. This annotation signifies that the principal has lost his capacity to give his agent the authority to act on his behalf.

Revocation is effective from the time of the act/ circumstance of the revocation.

Any actions taken by the Agent after the revocation, is an action taken after the principal loses his capacity and the Agent is in fact acting without authority. The only way an act of the agent can retain the validity at this point, is if it was concluded in good faith before the agent found out of the loss of capacity of the principal.

Renouncing/Surrendering a Power of Attorney

An agent can exercise the option to give up his position, if he no longer wishes to have the duty demanded by the office of agency. This can be done by the agent filing a notarized written document surrendering/renouncing the authority and having it recorded at the Deeds Registry. Once this document has been accepted by the Registry, the information will be annotated onto the Power indicating that the agent surrendered his authority and the document by which the power was surrendered.

Revocation or Surrendering Irrevocable Powers

If a Grantor or Agent wishes to revoke/renounce an irrevocable power they must, although not specifically stated, obtain proof of consent in writing of the other party mentioned in the power. Once consent is acquired the revocation/renunciation can be notarized, filed and recorded in the Deeds Registry. Once accepted by the Registry the change will be recorded on the Original document.

7. Irrevocable

"Very few things in life are irrevocable. Many decisions we make and actions are revocable, albeit with great difficulty and consequence."

– Anonymous

The Irrevocable power is a commercial instrument. While it bears the name "irrevocable power", it is not actually irrevocable. It is very difficult to revoke and requires the consent of both parties as mentioned earlier.

The reason that it is so difficult to revoke is that it was created to assist in agency transactions where one side requires absolute certainty that a commercial position will not change before a transaction is completed.

These instruments preserve the status quo and even break the normal rule of powers of attorney instruments formed under this Act; they are not limited by the capacity of the grantor. As such they can survive events that would usually cause the revocation of powers, such as, insanity, death, insolvency and bankruptcy.

Irrevocables under the law come in two distinct types:

- Irrevocable instruments given for valuable consideration[7].
- Irrevocable instruments for a fixed time[8].

The essence of the Irrevocable

No matter the type of irrevocable instrument, the following core elements remain the same.

First, the irrevocable instrument turns the usual formula on its head. Every other power is meant to safeguard the interests of the Grantor, the irrevocable safeguards the interests of the Agent.

---

[7] Section 6
[8] Section 7

Second, the instrument cannot be revoked unilaterally by the Grantor. The Agent must consent to the revocation.

Third, the instrument can survive the events that would usually strip it of its authority.

For Valuable Consideration

The essential element of the irrevocable circumscribed by valuable consideration is that the Agent must have paid in money or some other form of consideration for the privilege of binding the Grantor to keep the status quo until the transaction is completed.

Circumscribed by Time

The essential element for the irrevocable circumscribed by time, is that the power of the instrument can last no longer than a year.

8. Penalties

"Things gained through unjust fraud are never secure."

– Sophocles

Offences Surrounding Abuse of Powers of Attorney

A new feature of the Powers of Attorney Act circa 2022 is the addition of offences for using a Power for the Agent's gain or the gain of any other person. The Government of Guyana made the effort to insert two sections to combat, fraudulent sale and acquisition of land.

Offences committed by Agents

For this purpose, they have now included a section which penalizes an agent who obtains a power to benefit himself or another person or to cause loss to the grantor or another person.

Further the section penalizes an agent who didn't obtain the power for fraudulent purposes but goes on to use it for a fraudulent purpose, making it an offence to use a power to benefit himself or another person or to cause loss to the grantor or another person.

For any person who is found guilty of these criminal offenses the penalties if tried and convicted before the Magistrates Court is imprisonment for 5 years and a fine of 5 million GYD/ 24,000USD/20,000Euro/171,000Chinese Yuan/0.20Bitcoin. For a Corporate Entity convicted of this offence the penalty is 10 million GYD/48,000USD/40,000Euro/342,000ChineseYuan/0.40Bitcoin .

Notaries under the Spotlight

The legislation also makes a concerted effort to punish any unscrupulous notary, who may choose to assist an agent in any attempted fraudulent transaction. To this end, the Act creates several offences for Public Notaries.

Notaries failing to comply with duties of notarizing Powers of Attorney in Guyana

First, a Notary must comply with specific requirements for notarizing a power of attorney. Failure to comply is a strict liability offence. If any of the circumstances below occur and both the grantor and the agent are in Guyana, the notary can be charged and prosecuted:

i. The notary fails to have both parties appear before them with two forms of photo identification documents and a photocopy of each of the photo identification documents.

ii. The notary notarizes a document without the presence of both the Grantor and the Agent, even if one of them is present.

iii. The notary notarizes a document without being presented with both photo identification documents for both the Grantor and the Agent.

iv. The notary notarizes a document without the name and ID documents numbers being specified in the document.

v. The notary notarizes a document without the document being subscribed by two witnesses.

Notaries failing to comply with duties of notarizing Powers of Attorney outside Guyana

If a document is notarized outside of Guyana the same requirements apply. The Notary may be liable for prosecution if they fail to act in accordance with the five points listed above.

Documents notarized in Multiple Places

Sometimes because of the location of the parties to the Power of Attorney, the notarization needs to be done in two different countries. Even when it is done in different countries it must meet the following requirements. They are:

- A Notary must only notarize a document in the presence of the party to the document.
- A notary must only notarize a document upon being presented with both photo identification documents.

- A notary must only notarize a document with the name of the ID documents and the ID numbers being specified in the document.
- The notary must only notarize a document once the document has been subscribed by the two witnesses.

If a notary is found guilty of this criminal offense the penalties if tried and convicted before the Magistrates Court is imprisonment for 5 years and a fine of 5 million GYD/ 24,000USD/20,000Euro/171,000ChineseYuan/0.20Bitcoin.

Notaries conducting fraudulent transactions

A notary may also be found criminally liable for any actions which amounts to certifying or putting forward a false statement or fraudulently concealing, deceiving, withholding or perverting any fact or document pertaining to the power of attorney. This refers to situations where the agent may have co-opted the help of the Notary in his scheme to use the power of attorney given by a Grantor in breach of the agent's fiduciary duties.

If a notary is found guilty of this criminal offense the penalties if tried and convicted before the Magistrates Court is imprisonment for 5 years and a fine of 5 million GYD/24,000USD/20,000Euro/171,000ChineseYuan/0.20Bitcoin

.

Notaries conducting transactions while not permitted to practice

The final type of action that the Legislation seeks to punish is Notaries who are suspended or removed from the register of Public Notaries appointed by the President of the Co-operative Republic of Guyana from notarizing documents. Whether a suspended or removed notary purports to notarize a document for free or with a charge, he commits an offence.

If a notary is found guilty of this criminal offense the penalties if tried and convicted before the Magistrates Court is imprisonment for 5 years and a fine of 5 million GYD/ 24,000USD/20,000Euro/171,000ChineseYuan/0.20Bitcoin.

9. Updating & Instructions

"All business proceeds on beliefs, or judgements of probabilities, and not on certainties."

– Charles William Eliot

Perhaps one of the most confusing concepts to those dealing with Powers of Attorney is the concept of "updating" a Power.

This may give the impression that the Agent needs to be changed ever so often. While this may be a great idea for the sake of accountability of the agent, that is not the idea of updating in Guyana.

Updating a Power refers to the process of revisiting the Deeds Registry on a periodic basis to have a stamp imprinted on the power of Attorney which will indicate the instrument is still valid and has not been revoked by the Principal nor has it been revoked by operation of law.

Necessity

The process of updating a power is not set out in the Act, it is a procedure necessitated by the prevalence of fraudulent transactions. Please recall that when an instrument is recorded, it is always for the benefit of conducting transactions with third parties. Third parties that an agent has to transact business with on a principal's behalf are the parties who seek the comfort of the update stamp. To ensure that they are not being used in some unscrupulous scheme to defraud a principal.

Let us consider a common scenario, a power may be created where a principal authorizes his agent to carry out bank transactions on his behalf over a period of time. If those transactions were to occur a year after the power was recorded, the bank will ask the agent to update the Power with the Deeds Registry and return. This allows the bank to be sure that the agent still has the authority to act on behalf of his principal. It also confirms that the principal still has the capacity to allow the agent to act on his behalf. This will be an annual feature as long as the power exists.

For the avoidance of doubt, a power of attorney should be updated annually. The organizations that an agent will be interfacing with will require the updating, whether that organization is Governmental or Private Sector.

Carrying Instructions

A Principal should prepare notes of instruction to be sent via email to the Agent. The Agent should in turn provide the note with the power in carrying out a specific task. This will make the agents' tasks significantly easier if the places they visit to complete the tasks see a note emanating from the principal. In a society where institutions have an acquired distrust for the use of powers, given the nefarious purpose they are sometimes used for, carrying instructions is the soul of prudence.

Part III – Cautionary Tenets

10. The Burden of Agency

"Within the hearts of some men, loyalty and consideration are esteemed greater than success"

– Bryant H McGill

The concept of Loyal Service

As mentioned previously, the language that is used in Guyana to discuss Agency needs to change. It needs to move from reflecting favours asked, to that of a duty being handled with loyalty and commitment.

For the misuse of agency instruments to decrease, the knowledge of the duties of an agent must become widespread. It should also be included at the end of the legislation as a schedule, which would set out all the duties of the parties.

The duties should also be printed on the Power of Attorney document. This way a grantor and agent who read the document would have an opportunity to see what they are agreeing to, before signing the document. Also this will at least make all but the most seasoned fraudsters, think twice before taking advantage of their position of authority.

The List of 12 Duties

Below are compiled all the common law duties of a Agent. They are listed in no particular order:

Loyalty

The agent has a fiduciary duty[9] to act loyally for the principal's benefit, in the matters set out in the Power of Attorney instrument.[10]

---

[9] See Footnote 3 and 4

[10] Restatement of Agency (Third Edn)

Taking reasonable care

The agent needs to understand that he must exercise the same care, competence and diligence as a reasonable person would exercise in his own affairs. He must be able to act reasonably and carefully; if he cannot do so, he should not accept the duty of an agent.

Not to acquire material benefit from the Agency

Agents must not acquire material benefit for themselves or any third parties.

Not to act for Parties with adverse interests

An agent must not act on behalf of persons with an interest adverse to those of their principal. This duty should be obvious to any reasonable person, as in my opinion this is a variation of the loyalty principle.

Not to Compete

This is particularly important for Agency in a business context. An agent cannot use a power, or the information gained during his tenure as an agent to compete with the principal or assist the principal's competitors. Once the agency has run it's course the agent may take the decision to become a competitor. However he must take particular care not to breach his fiduciary duties or any contractual non-disclosure or non-compete provisions.

Use of the Principal's property

It is deeply egregious for an agent to use the property of the principal for his own benefit.

Keeping the Principal's confidence

It is fundamental that an agent does not share any confidential information shared by his principal to any third party. This may be covered in a contractual situation by non-disclosure or non-compete provisions. For those agency agreements not covered by contractual terms, this principle is important to remember.

Acting within the scope of the Authority

A breach of this duty is a fundamental breach of trust between Principal and Agent. To act outside the scope is to usurp the power which was never conferred on the agent. This can cause serious reputational, possibly even pecuniary harm to a principal.

Following Lawful Instructions

There are two things to note about this duty, the requirement to follow instructions and that only lawful instructions are to be followed.

Power of Attorney instruments, almost always have a provision that authorizes the Agent to take any further action directed by the principal in written communication. This is especially useful as any authority that does not appear on the face of the instrument will need to be verified in written form by the principal.

The agent when he decides to step into the shoes of the principal must appreciate that receiving further tasks is a possibility. Once they choose to remain an agent, they are duty bound to carry out the task, unless the tasks violate the law. If an agent is given a lawful task to carry out, they must do so unless they can get the principal to relent or they choose to renounce their position as agent.

Providing Information

The agent has a duty to keep his principal well informed on the execution of his responsibilities.

Being Prudent

This is a commonsense duty for any man of business – be prudent in your affairs. An agent must refrain from taking imprudent decisions in the affairs he has agreed to conclude for the principal. The test for this duty would be determining what a reasonable man would do in the situation.

Accounting

Lack of accountability is the fertilizer that helps fraud grow strong. To ensure his loyalty in this position of trust he has tripartite duties set out below:

Segregation of Assets

The Agent must not mingle his principal's property with his own.

Appearances

The agent should not deal with his principal's property as to give the impression it is his own.

Records

An agent must keep records and accounts, which must be able to be produced relating to the money or other property received or paid out on the principal's account.

11. A Principal's Diligence

"The cautious seldom err"

– Confucius

The principal/agent relationship is not without duties on the principal's side, although the duties on the agent's side are considerably greater.

The Principal has 3 critical duties to be diligent and act in good faith. If a principal lapses in observing his duties it can cause the breakdown or bring an end to the Agency. They are the following:

Dealing fairly with the Agent in good faith

The principal has asked the agent to conclude matters on his behalf, with or without remuneration, it must be on a basis of mutual respect. As such the principal must parley with the agent in good faith, fully explaining to the chosen agent the following particulars, before an instrument is executed or recorded:

- The extent of the assignment/s.
- The risk that may come with the assignment, if any.
- The chance of monetary loss or physical harm that the agent may be exposed to in the course of the agency.
- The cost, if any, that the agent may incur and the plan for reimbursement.
- Provide the agent with access to documents, resources and access to funds that may be required.

Reimbursement and Indemnification of the Agent

When a principal asks an agent to take on business on his behalf, he must be willing to reimburse the agent for payments made on his behalf.

If the agent should suffer any loss, which should be rightly borne by the principal, he must be indemnified by the principal.

This duty is not without limitation. An agent can only be reimbursed or indemnified for payments or losses that arose within the scope of the agent's authority. Payments must have benefited the principal. Any loss must have been made officiously by the agent.

Acting according to the terms of the Agency

The principal just like the agent has a duty to honour the clear terms of the agreement, that have established the relationship.

The principal should not act in bad faith and expand the scope of the agency agreement without discussing the matter with the agent with the aim of getting his consent to conduct further transactions.

12. Necessary Action

"Be prudent in your affairs or suffer the loss of time, money and opportunity"

– Anonymous

The Need for Agency Contracts

From what I have witnessed as an Attorney-at-Law practicing in Guyana, the granting of a Power is treated as a favour, rather than the commercial transaction it is.

As this text shows it should not be considered a favour to complete "one or two fine things" for a family member or close friend. In most cases the instrument may as well be an employment contract. Most times the favour you are asked to do can amount to a full-time job without remuneration.

If the power is granted in the context of a job within the scope of that job's description, then that is acceptable. But if it is outside of a job or a job description and it is onerous in terms of time and resources, the agent should be compensated.

This may be an unpopular position with a principal. As part of the culture in Guyana is to get the most out of a situation while giving as little of your resources as possible. Principals will probably be opposed to such an idea. It is incumbent on the agent to press the topic as the burden falls on the agent's shoulders.

Greater Education needed for both Principals and Agents

The duties and responsibilities of principals and agents are hardly known. If fraud and mala fides dealing is to be stemmed, the lack of knowledge has to change. A book like this is helpful, but widespread public education is the only remedy for this problem.

Need for the Duties to be included in the Instrument

It would have a strong psychological effect on both principal and agent to have the duties included in the power of attorney instrument itself. This would make both sides think twice about taking action which would breach their duties and responsibilities.

Having the duties as part of the signed document would also be useful. It would be conclusive evidence of the guilty mind of the person who uses a Power for the commission of fraudulent transactions. Such evidence would offer critical support for any person who wants to bring such an alleged perpetrator to justice or recover money or property through the Courts.

Appendix

The Powers of Attorneys Act

(Consolidated up to March 2026)

ARRANGEMENT OF SECTIONS

An Act to make provision with respect to the recording of Powers of Attorney, their effect and their revocation.

Short Title

1. This Act may be cited as the Powers of Attorney Act.

Interpretation

2. In this Act—

"property" includes immovable and movable property, and any debt, and any thing in action, and any other right or interest in the nature of property, whether in possession or not;

"purchaser" includes a lessee or mortgagee, or an intending purchaser, lessee or mortgagee, or other person, who, for valuable consideration, takes or deals for property, and "purchase" has a meaning corresponding with that of purchaser.

Power of Attorney

2A. (1) An instrument creating a power of attorney shall be executed with the donor of the power and the donee of the power appearing personally together before a Public Notary or Magistrate as the law may require, and the donor and done shall each provide the Public Notary or Magistrate with two photograph identification documents that establish their identity and a photocopy of each documents.

(2) Where the donor is out of Guyana and the donee is in Guyana, the donor and the donee shall each appear personally before a Public Notary or Magistrate, as the law may require, in the country in which he is and execute the power of attorney, providing the Public Notary or Magistrate with two photograph identification documents that establish his identity and a photocopy of each document.

(3) The Power of Attorney shall specify the name and number of every identification document of the donor and donee.

(4) The power of attorney shall be signed by the donor and donee in the presence of a Public Notary or Magistrate and two witnesses, and subscribed by the witnesses in the presence of each other before being signed, sealed or stamped by the Public Notary or Magistrate:

Provided that where a donor executes the power of attorney out of Guyana, a separate witness statement shall be given by one of the subscribing witnesses.

(5) The power of attorney shall not be registered, filed or recorded in the Deeds Registry, unless the power of attorney has attached to it copies of the two photograph identification documents, bio-data page in the case of a passport, of the donor and donee, and a separate witness statement given under subsection (4), which have been certified, signed and sealed or stamped by a Public Notary or Magistrate.

(6) For the purposes of this section identification documents include, a national identification card, a valid passport and a valid driver's license.

Power of Attorney to be recorded

3. A power of attorney, including a power ad lites or a special power providing for the passing of a transport, or for the execution or assignment of a particular mortgage or lease or for the cancellation of a mortgage, or a power providing for the obtaining or recording of probate or letters of administration and for no other purpose, whether made within or without the limits of Guyana, together with the attached copies of the two photograph identification documents of the donor and the donee and the witness statements referred to in section 2A(5), shall be proved and filed as of record or proved and recorded in the Deeds Registry, and an act done in pursuance of such a power shall not be valid, and such a power shall not be admitted in evidence in any suit, action or other proceeding unless the same be

proved and filed as of record, or proved and recorded, in the Deeds Registry.

Execution under Power of Attorney

4. (1) The donee of a power of attorney may, if he thinks fit, execute or do any assurance, instrument, or thing in and with his own name and signature, and under his own seal, where sealing is required, by the authority of the donor of the power; and every assurance, instrument, and thing so executed and done shall be as effectual in law, to all intents, as if it had been executed or done by the donee of the power in the name and with the signature and seal of the donor thereof.

(2) This section applies to powers of attorney created by instruments executed either before or after the commencement of this Act.

Payment by Attorney under power without notice of death

5. (1) Any person making any payment or doing any act, in good faith, in pursuance of a power of attorney, shall not be liable in respect of the payment or act by

reason that before the payment or act the donor of the power had died or become subject to disability or insolvent, or had revoked the power, if the fact of death, disability, insolvency or revocation was not at the time of the payment or act known to the person making or doing the same.

(2) A statutory declaration by an attorney to the effect that he has not received any notice or information of the revocation of such power of attorney by death or otherwise shall, if made immediately before or within three months after any such payment or act as aforesaid, be taken to be conclusive proof of such non-revocation at the time when such payment or act was made or done. Where the donee of the power of attorney is a corporation aggregate, the officer appointed to act for the corporation in the execution of the power may make the statutory declaration in like manner as if that officer

had been the donee of the power. Where probate or letters of administration have been granted to any person, as attorney for some other person, this section applies as if the payment made or acts done under the grant had been made or done under a power of attorney.

(3) This section does not affect any right against the payee of any person interested in any money so paid; and that person shall have the like remedy against the payee as he would have had against the payer if the payment had not been made by him.

(4) This section applies to payments and acts made and done before or after the commencement of this Act.

Effect of irrevocable power of attorney for value

6. If a power of attorney given for valuable consideration is in the instrument creating the power

expressed to be irrevocable, then, in favour of a purchaser—

(a) the power shall not be revoked at any time either by anything done by the donor of the power without the concurrence of the donee of the power, or by the death, disability or insolvency of the donor of the power; and

(b) any act done at any time by the donee of the power in pursuance of the power shall be as valid as if anything done by the donor of the power without the concurrence of the donee of the power, or the death, disability or insolvency of the donor of the power, had not been done or happened; and

(c) neither the donee of the power nor the purchaser shall at any time be prejudicially affected by notice of anything done by the donor of the power without the concurrence of the donee of the power, or of the death, disability or insolvency of the donor of the power.

Effect of power of attorney irrevocable for a fixed time.

7. If a power of attorney, whether given for valuable consideration or not, is in the instrument creating the power expressed to be irrevocable for a fixed time therein specified, not exceeding one year from the date of the instrument, then in favour of a purchaser—

(a) the power shall not be revoked for and during that fixed time either by anything done by the donor of the power without the concurrence of the donee of the power, or by the death, disability or insolvency of the donor of the power; and

(b) any act done within that fixed time by the donee of the power in pursuance of the power shall be as valid as if anything done by the donor of the power without the concurrence of the donee of the power, or the death, disability or insolvency of the donor of the power, had not been done or

happened; and

(c) neither the donee of the power, nor the purchaser, shall at any time be prejudicially affected by notice either during or after that fixed time of anything done by the donor of the power during the fixed time without the concurrence of the donee of the power, or of the death, disability, or insolvency of the donor of the power, within that fixed time.

Devolution of power of attorney given to a purchaser

8. A power of attorney given for valuable consideration may be given to a purchaser of property or any interest therein, and to the persons deriving title under him thereto, and those persons shall be the duly constituted attorneys for all the purposes of the power, but without prejudice to any right to appoint substitutes given by the power.

Power of attorney granted by married woman

9. A married woman has power, as if she were unmarried and of full age, by deed to appoint an attorney on her behalf for the purpose of executing any deed or doing any other act which she might herself

Duration of recorded power

execute or do, and the provisions of this Act relating to instruments creating powers of attorney apply thereto.

10. A power of attorney, not falling within the provisions of sections 5 and 6 hereof, heretofore or hereafter recorded in the Deeds Registry, shall, unless a contrary intention appears therein, continue in force until the revocation thereof by the principal shall be recorded or an entry is made thereon as hereinafter provided; and every act, deed or instrument of the attorney after revocation and before the revocation is recorded or an entry is made shall be valid in favour of any person bona fide and without notice of revocation dealing with the attorney in the name of the principal.

Revocation of power

11. A power of attorney may be revoked by the filing as of record or the recording in the Deeds Registry of a deed or other instrument revoking the same, or by an entry in writing under the hand of the Registrar or the Deputy Registrar on a power recorded in the Registry

of the death, lunacy, unsoundness of mind or insolvency of the principal, upon evidence by statutory declaration sufficient to satisfy the Registrar or Deputy Registrar of such death or disability.

Offences to dishonestly obtain and use a power of attorney.

12(1) A person shall not dishonestly obtain a power of attorney –

(a) to obtain financial advantage for the person or another person; or

(b) to cause loss to the principal or another person.

(2) An attorney under a power of attorney shall not dishonestly use the power of attorney –

(a) to obtain financial advantage for the attorney or another person; or

(b) to cause loss to the donor of the power or another person.

(3) An attorney who fails to comply with this subsection commits an offence and is liable on summary conviction to a fine of five million dollars and to imprisonment for five years; and in the case of a body corporate ten million dollars.

(4) In this section a reference to a power of attorney included a reference to a power of attorney that is invalid or has been revoked.

Other offences

13(1) If any Public Notary who is suspended or removed from practice or whose name is not on the register, whether for reward or not, makes, does or exercises or performs any act, matter or thing pertaining or belonging to the office, function or practice of Public Notary commits an offence.

(2) A person who willfully certifies or propounds any false statement or document, or who fraudulently, with intent to deceive, conceals, withholds or perverts

any fact or document pertinent to the subject of a power of attorney commits an offence.

(3) A person who fails to comply with any of the duties imposed on the person under section 2A commits an offence.

(4) A person who commits an offence under this section is liable on summary conviction to a fine of five million dollars and to imprisonment for five years.

Regulations

14. The Minister may make regulations as may be necessary for the better carrying out the provisions of the Act.

SCHEDULE 1

Regulations made under

the Powers of Attorney Act

IN EXERCISE OF THE POWERS CONFERRED UPON ME BY SECTION 14 OF THE POWERS OF ATTORNEY ACT, I MAKE THE FOLLOWING REGULATIONS: -

1. These regulations may be cited as the Powers of Attorney regulations 2022.

Form of identification documents

2. The copies of the photograph identification documents that establish the identities of the donor and done of a power of attorney, provided to the Deeds Registry to be filed or recorded with a power of attorney in the Deeds Registry shall be clear and in colour, and certified, signed and sealed or stamped by the Public Notary or Magistrate as true copies of the original documents of the donor and donee.

Saving of extant powers of attorney

3. For the avoidance of doubt all powers of attorney filed and recorded in the Deeds Registry before the commencement of the Powers of Attorney (Amendment) Act 2022 and the Deeds Registry (Amendment) Act 2022 shall remain valid and subsisting.

Made in the USA
Monee, IL
05 November 2026

67808926R00046